LEARN TO WRITE CSS THE AW

I0004554

CSS

"Awesomeness Book"

GILAD E TSUR-MAYER

CSS Awesomeness Book

Learn To Write CSS the Awesome Way

Gilad E. Tsur Mayer

Table of Contents

Stop Everything! I Have a Present For You!

OMG! OMG! OMG!! Aren't you excited?! I *love* presents!

This book will help you learn CSS, but personally I prefer videos over books (since it's easier if someone does all the work of reading for you, don't you think?) You can watch a bunch of videos and in no time you will be an expert.

So, I took this book, and blended it all into a bite-sized video course. If you will watch it, you will know every basic building block of CSS in no time! Neat, huh?

And because you have purchased *this* book, I will give you 50% off this video course. Awesome, right?

So, what are you waiting for? Grab the videos here: http://basiccss.gilad.me/discount50/

Introduction

Hey Guys!

Welcome to the CSS Awesomeness Course, where you will learn to write the basics of CSS, the awesome way.

My name is Gilad, and I will lead you through this amazing course!

Even before I was a cartoon character, I began my career as a web developer. Soon afterward, I transitioned to entrepreneurship and founded my very own startup company.

Currently, I work at the company I've founded from scratch, and also I do what I love the most: teaching you guys!

I designed this course for anyone seeking to learn basic CSS and begin a career as a rockstar web developer (as well as anybody who just loves to expand their knowledge.)

By the end of the course, you will have a rock-solid knowledge of all CSS building blocks such as:

- Selectors
- Width & height
- The box model
- CSS backgrounds
- And many, many more...

Oh! We will even learn how to use the almighty developer tools!

I will teach you the latest version of CSS3 by the standards of the W3C Association. These standards are used by all the major companies in the world.

Not only will I cover all of these topics, but I will also give you an opportunity to practice them by giving you a pop quiz every now and then.

The ideal student for this course is anybody who wants to expand their knowledge of CSS or get a leg up in the web developer world.

The only prerequisites necessary to enroll is a basic knowledge of HTML and an open-mind to my silly jokes!

You are free to take a look at the course description, and I look forward to meeting you inside.

Why learn CSS anyway ?

When I first learned about web development, I wanted to build the next big thing in the internet world, which is clearly: *Green Stripes Racoon Website.*

I armed myself with a bit of HTML knowledge and started out immediately!

I added a snippet of code here, a little bit of HTML there, and voila!!..

My website looked hideous! (yay!)

I stepped back a bit, and then looked at other big websites out there. I noticed that they were using awesome colors, fonts and borders.. and lots of other tricks I didn't know about.

I investigated for a whole…. 2 seconds and discovered they were using a magical code language: "CSS." Oh wow..

In this second, I knew my life purpose for the next week: learning CSS (*the awesome way...*)

There are more reasons to learn CSS, for sure...like adding cool animations, being mobile-friendly, and even customizing your content more easily.

We will cover ALL of those in this course...and I will make sure you will get your dose of bad jokes!

What is CSS?

CSS is shorthand for Cascading Style Sheets (leave it to the marketing dudes...) and quite boldly in charge of all the design of your document.

If HTML is the big guy who is in charge of the structure, then CSS is the hipster designer who loves to make everything pretty.

It will make your fonts, colors, margins, borders, height and width, background images and all the pretty stuff you can think of..

Do I need to know anything before I write CSS?

Although it's a CSS course, we will use HTML in this course, as well. So, before diving into this book, you will need to arm yourself with a little bit of HTML knowledge.

We will write down the structure of our examples through HTML and then design it with our awesomely new CSS skills!

For all my examples in this course I will use Notepad++, which is a completely free text editor.

(by the way, you can grab it here : http://notepad-plus-plus.org/download)

However, if you are happen to be allergic to my suggestions, you can always try other software.

I won't judge you, i promise!

whispering I will!... ***whispering***

Set up your CSS

In CSS we have several ways to place our styling inside of our project.

The most *unhealthy* way, is the inline method:

```
<p style="CSS CODE"> My Zebra has no legs..
</p>
```

As you can see, we have a style attribute, then in the value of the attribute, we have our CSS code. This method is not ideal. Let me set an example, so you will see why:

```
<p style="SAME CSS CODE"> My Zebra has no
legs.. </p>
<p style="SAME CSS CODE"> But it has </p>
<p style="SAME CSS CODE">.. </p>
```

You can see that you clearly have a problem here, since you wrote the same CSS code 3 times.

If you are a lazy person like myself, let's see how you can solve this problem using the other method we've got :

```
<!DOCTYPE html>
<html>
    <head>
        <title> Zebra Website </title>
        <style>
            ..CSS CODE TO CLASS..
```

```
        </style>
    </head>

    <body>
        <p class="CSS CONNECTED"> My Zebra has
        no legs.. </p>
        <p class="CSS CONNECTED"> But it has
        </p>
        <p class="CSS CONNECTED"> .. </p>
    </body>
</html>
```

In this example, we can see that we cleared all the unhealthy inline CSS method from the *p* tag and replaced it with a class, then connected just *one* CSS code in the style tag, up in the head tag.

So eventually we saved a bit of energy by only making our statement once.

Uh-oh!!... We've got another lazy-problem...

Let's say we set our home page with the kind of CSS we just wrote , and then we want to write another page, say .. our "contact us" with the same CSS code?

We would need to write down *all* of our CSS code *again* ?! Geez! Too much work for me, sir!

In this case, we've got another trick up our sleeve: CSS *external link.* We will make a new file with a ".css" extension, then link it to every webpage in which we want our CSS to take place:

7

```
<head>
    <link rel="stylesheet" type="text/css"
    href="style.css" />
</head>
```

On the "href" attribute, write your file path, and that's how you set up your page (*the awesome way...*)

CSS Selectors

♫ .. We are going to learn some.. CSS..Selectors... Woo...Hoo... ♫

So.. what do you say about my CSS Selector song, huh? Pretty-pretty .. amazing, eh?

I was thinking about submitting it to MTV's Top 10 one of these days and beating Justin Bieber! That would be a great day...to humanity, even.

Anyway, CSS Selector! Yes!

This is the day you are going to learn one of the greatest (and most valuable) lessons you can learn in CSS building blocks: CSS Selectors.

What is CSS Selector? Selector is (quite self-explanatory) a CSS way to select your HTML Element and say to your browser, "Alright browser, would you be a sport, and grab this element for me? Oh, then make it blue!"

The structure of the Selector is very easy: first (optional,) we have our type of selector (most of the time, beginning with ID or CLASS selectors;) then we have the name of the selector; next, we open our curly brackets; inside, we have our CSS declarations!

The declarations are made of property and value. We take each declaration apart with a colon sign, and end each with a semicolon.

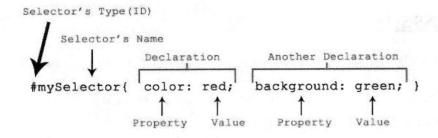

That's it! That's all you need to know about CSS Selectors. And my CSS selector song, of course.. ♫ ..CSS..Selectors... Woo .. Hoo... ♫

ID Selector & Class Selector

In this example we introduce the selector type ID, but we also have a Class Selector.

What is the difference between them, you ask ?

Imagine that we are having 3 *p* elements in our document.

Each and every one of them represents a member of my least favorite family in the whole world: The Kardashian Family!

Let's write it down in our text editor:

```
<p >Kim </p>
<p >Rob </p>
<p >Kourtney </p>
```

Now, we can call them by their names: Kim, Rob, Kourtney (with a K, of kourse..) By doing so, we are accessing a particular member of the Kardashian family, and we can attach an id attribute:

```
<p id="kim">Kim </p>
<p id="rob">Rob </p>
<p id="kourtney">Kourtney </p>
```

So if we want to, let's say, lock Kim in a border, we can select Kim's ID, and create a border around her name.

```
#kim{
    border: 1px solid red;
}
```

But, if we would like to make borders of *all* the Kardashian's family member? Will we select all of them by name?! Nahh.. we are too lazy for that task, aren't we?!

Instead, we would add a class attribute for them!

Like that :

```
<p id="kim" class="kardashian">Kim </p>
<p id="rob" class="kardashian">Rob </p>
<p id="kourtney" class="kardashian">Kourtney
</p>
```

Now we will edit our CSS file:

```
.kardashian{
    border: 1px solid green;
}
```

Note the difference between class and ID- if we want to access a class, we have that little dot, and if we want to access an id, we have that pound sign..

Easy, huh?

Now we can lock all the Kardashians in our shiny red border.. And this hard task is achieved only with one snippet of code!!

Our very own first project

Do you remember a few lessons ago, I told you about my first attempt to build the next big thing on the internet which is the *Green Stripes Racoon Website*? Do you??

Well, today we will try again to achieve this kind of world wide recognition and build our first *Green Stripes Racoon Website*!

So before we do, we will setup our project real nice, create a css folder in the main folder, and create a .css file called "style." Then, in your main folder, create an .html file called "index." Inside of it, type:

```
<!DOCTYPE html>
<html>
    <head>
        <title> </title>
        <link rel="stylesheet" type="text/css"
        href="style.css" />
    </head>

    <body>

    </body>
</html>
```

Now we are all set! Let's get started!

By the way, just because I'm making the *Green Stripes Racoon Website*, doesn't mean you can't make whatever website you want!

What kind of website are *you* making? Type your answer in the Q and A section in Udemy, and share it with me!.

CSS width and height

First thing in our Green Racoon website, is ... to have a Green navigation top.

So, let's create a Div Element.

A Div Element is acting like a section within our HTML, and we can manipulate it quite smoothly with our CSS skills.

I'll create a div:

```
<div> </div>
```

Then, I want to define its width and height, so I will create a class attribute, and call it "top-nav":

```
<div class="top-nav"> </div>
```

And inside my css file, I want my top navigation bar to be very wide (side to side,) and the height to be 90 pixels.

so I will write this down::

```
.top-nav {
    width: 100%;
    height: 90px;
}
```

Save it, refresh it, and voila... nothing shows.. What gives?!

Maybe because we don't have any color for our top navigation bar?

Backgrounds

To make our green div pop, we will need to color it (with the color green, I guess..)

In your css file, add to your top-nav class this line:

```
background-color: green;
```

If you want to be more particular, you can, instead, go with a hexadecimal color like this:

```
background-color: #F296D7;
```

By the way, I use the *colorpicker.com* website, if you want to be more *picky* with your colors.

We can also get a background image, like this:

```
background-image: url('../img/bg.jpg');
```

And that's how you do backgrounds!

Cool , huh?!

CSS box model (and a bonus! Al... right!)

If you will save your document and refresh your page, you can clearly see that we have a margin right on our "top-nav" class.

And that's due to our css box-model.

Now, bear with me, because most of the people who learn this thing tend to kill themselves in this lesson. My students, in particular, try to do so after they hear one of my jokes, coming just *before* they are introduced to the box model. Therefore, I never learn how they would react to the box model. Nevertheless, I'll try to do my best:

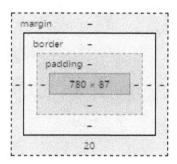

For this demonstration, I will get the hand of the mandatory *p* tag. Let's write inside of it: "I've got a feeling we are not in Kansas Anymore" with a "toto" id.

```
<p id="toto"> I've got a feeling we are not
in Kansas Anymore </p>
```

Almost every element in HTML has a secret 4 layers inside of it. We have our content, which is our text (the first layer.)

Let's have it colored yellow ....just to make it pop out of the screen.

```
#toto{background-color: yellow;  }
```

To this text we can add a green *border* (the second layer), 3 pixels wide solid line.

```
#toto{background-color: yellow; border: 3px
solid green;}
```

Now we have 2 more of both sides of the border, we have the *padding* layer, which lies on the inner side of the border,

```
#toto{
    background-color: yellow;
    border: 3px solid green;
    padding: 20px;
}
```

And also the *margin*, which lies on the outer side of the border.

```
#toto{
    background-color: yellow;
    border: 3px solid green;
    margin: 20px;
    padding: 20px;
}
```

That's it! That wasn't so bad, was it ?

Now to address our problem earlier, all we need to do is place a margin:0; to our body element (because our browser has a preset of margin and padding for some reason..,) and we are good to go!

```
body{ margin: 0; }
```

Here's a useful tip!

If you are on PC, using Chrome , Firefox or even IE, you can press F12, then hover the cursor over your own code lines through your browser. They will show you really great input! Also, you can play around with your CSS and HTML code *in your browser!* Impressive, huh?

CSS float (and other stuff..)

Now that we have our Top Navigation set and ready, we should populate it with a little bit of flair.

Let's say we want to have banner and a logo...and navigation buttons...and a squirrel (you know, just in case!)

So let's just say we want three divs to represent every section we need: logo, banner, navigation. Then, order them horizontally.

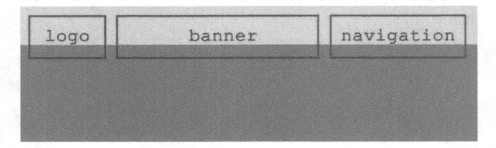

Let's try this one:

```
<div class="logo" ></div>
<div class="banner"></div>
<div class="nav-wrapper"></div>
```

Now we will set width and height for each and every one of them. Also, for the sake of being sane, let's color them in different colors, so we can see them on the screen. We will change the color afterwards.

```
.logo{width: 250px; height: 90px;background-color: green; }
```

```
.banner{width: 350px; height:
90px;background-color: yellow; }
  .nav-wrapper{width: 370px; height:
90px;background-color: orange; }
```

WHAT?? Oh, man... what gives?! How come my divs decided to stack on each other like a bunch of bananas?

Well.. that's because divs behavior, by default, is to take all of the width they've got, so the next div in line is under the last one and so on.. How can we resolve that ?

Enters .. *float*! *trumpets*

With float you can push your element to one side...and make room for the other.

Add `float: left;` to your *logo* and *banner*, and `float: right;` to the *nav-wrapper*.

And... yeah, baby! We've got it!

And now we can erase the ugly *background color* that we've got for draft..

Now, let's try to take care of our navigation buttons.

We want to create three buttons and order them horizontally, then design them a bit.

So let's create three unordered list items, with a link inside of our *nav-wrapper* div.

```
<div class="nav-wrapper">
```

```
<ul>
    <li>
        <a href="index.html" class="nav-
        btn">Homepage</a>
    </li>
    <li>
        <a href="gallery.html" class="nav-
        btn">Racoon's
        Gallery</a>
    </li>
    <li>
        <a href="contact.html" class="nav-
        btn">
        Contact a random Racoon</a>
    </li>
</ul>
</div>
```

Now we can style them a bit:

First thing first! I have the weirdly bullets that come as bundle with the list items, so I will have them erased. I will select the ul tag directly, and then write *list-style-type* as *none*, and bam!

Gone! I'm awesome, I tell you!

Then, we will set our *nav-btn* with a little bit of *padding* to have our buttons with a lil' bit of fluff. We will color it with a bit of greenish color.

I'll set all of the buttons with float left, so they will order horizontally, and maybe add to all of them a lil' bit of margin left so they will have spaces between them.

And maybe ... have the text color white with a lil' bit of border on the bottom of the buttons, to add a bit of flair..

```
.nav-btn{
    padding:5px;
    background-color: #e698a5;
    float: left;
    text-decoration: none;
    margin-left: 10px;
    color: white;
    border-bottom: 2px solid #c74E80;
}

ul{ list-style-type: none;}
```

What do you say about that, huh ?

Our *Green Stripes Racoon* website navigation is all set!

CSS fonts

I'm getting the feeling that we're not really happy with the font we are having here..

So to fix that, we need to understand what we want.

We want our website to be consistent with its font, so we will select the body element, and type font-family: arial;

```
body{ font-family: arial; }
```

Let's program together!

That was so much fun!

I had a blast!!

Now that you know the building blocks of CSS, you can continue yourself and try to use all the stuff we just learned.

By the way, there are many properties in CSS, more than we can think of, so I'm leaving you a free cheat sheet with a huge amount of CSS properties and what they can do for you.

Now what ?

Congratulations!

You accomplished this course, you heard lots of bad jokes in this book, and yet you've made it! I'm very proud of you!

You might ask yourself:

Now that I've accomplished my first CSS course, what should I do? How can I improve my web developing skills? Well, my young padawan, it's now time to combine your HTML and CSS skills with some Javascript!

I do have a Javascript course just for you, and because you purchased this book (or in compensation for my bad jokes,) I will give you 50% off all of my courses in Udemy.

Just email me at: http://basiccss.gilad.me/discount50/ and ask for the discount!

CSS PROPERTIES

Color Properties:

Property	Description	Browsers
color	Sets the color of text	all
opacity	Sets the opacity level for an element	Newer only

Background properties:

Property	Description	Browsers
background	A shorthand property for setting all the background properties in one declaration	all
background-color	Specifies the background color of an element	all
background-image	Specifies one or more background images for an element	all
background-position	Specifies the position of a background image	all
background-repeat	Sets how a background image will be repeated	all

Borders properties:

Property	Description	Browsers
border	*Sets all the border properties in one declaration*	all
border-bottom	*Sets a border in the bottom of the element*	all
border-top	*Sets a border in the top of the element*	all
border-right	*Sets a border on the right of the element*	all
border-left	*Sets a border on the left of the element*	all
border-radius	*Makes your border's element curvy*	Newer only

Box properties:

Property	Description	Browsers
width	*Sets the width of an element*	all
height	*Sets the height of an element*	all
bottom	*Specifies the bottom position of a positioned element*	all
top	*Specifies the top position of a positioned element*	all
left	*Specifies the left position of a positioned element*	all
right	*Specifies the right position of a positioned element*	all
display	*Specifies if a certain HTML element will be displayed*	all
float	*Specifies whether or not a box should float*	all

margin	Sets all the margin properties in one declaration	all
margin-bottom	Sets the bottom margin of an element	all
margin-top	Sets the bottom margin of an element	all
margin-left	Sets the left margin of an element	all
margin-right	Sets the right margin of an element	all
padding	Sets all the padding properties in one declaration	all
padding-bottom	Sets the bottom padding of an element	all
padding-top	Sets the top padding of an element	all
padding-left	Sets the left padding of an element	all
padding-right	Sets the right padding of an element	all

Text and Font properties:

Property	Description	Browsers
text-align	Specifies the horizontal alignment of text	all
text-decoration	Specifies the decoration added to text	all
word-spacing	Increases or decreases the space between words in a text	all
font-family	Specifies the font family for text	all
font-size	Specifies the font size for text	all
font-weight	Specifies the weight of a font	all

www.ingramcontent.com/pod-product-compliance
Lightning Source LLC
Chambersburg PA
CBHW070928050326
40689CB00015B/3667